THE GOOD DARK

*

THE GOOD DARK

Annie Guthrie

Tupelo Press
North Adams, Massachusetts

THE GOOD DARK.
Text copyright © 2015 Annie Guthrie. All rights reserved. Foreword copyright ©
2015 Dan Beachy-Quick. All rights reserved.

Library of Congress Cataloging-in-Publication Data

Guthrie, Annie.
 [Poems. Selections]
 The good dark / Annie Guthrie. – First paperback edition.
    pages cm
 ISBN 978-1-936797-59-2 (pbk. : alk. paper)
 I. Title.
 PS3607.U7983A6 2015
 811'.6–dc23
                    2015028309

Cover designed by Annie Guthrie. Text designed and set in New Caledonia
by Howard Klein.
Cover photograph: "Man, Pinacate, Sonora," by Rosanna Salonia.
Used with permission (www.fotovitamina.com).

First paperback edition: October 2015.

Tupelo Press
P.O. Box 1767, North Adams, Massachusetts 01247
Telephone: (413) 664–9611
editor@tupelopress.org / www.tupelopress.org

Tupelo Press is an award-winning independent literary press that publishes fine
fiction, nonfiction, and poetry in books that are a joy to hold as well as read. Tupelo
Press is a registered 501(c)(3) nonprofit organization, and we rely on public support
to carry out our mission of publishing extraordinary work that may be outside the
realm of the large commercial publishers. Financial donations are welcome and are
tax deductible.

for Tommaso

Contents

Why am I a little girl
Where am I a little girl
When I am a little girl
Which little girl am I

— Gertrude Stein

Foreword

If not exactly comfort, I've long taken refuge in Ralph Waldo Emerson's thought that the truest rule of the universe entire is compensation. Not, of course, that base form of compensation in which one's work is rewarded with easier satisfactions: money, renown, award. No, I mean those forms of compensation so subtle they complicate our notion of what is properly due. Against that lovely mystic simplicity—"as above, so below"—I might suggest reciprocity comes riddled with its own generosity. One labors in the field not simply to receive the grain's harvest, but because the work itself invites that gift work alone cannot earn: art, energy, some fundamental recognition of a world that keeps itself in relation to the one who seeks it, and who in seeking, ends by finding herself as one whom by the world is sought.

Annie Guthrie is a poet involved in just such labor, and her book *The Good Dark*, offers itself as a curious testament to the labyrinthine complexity of human relation to the world and those others that fill it. For in the poems there are powers, there are forces, there are laws, but none of them exert an authority that removes the poet from her need to write so as to listen: "sometimes it admits you its existence." That existence is manifold. There is nature, and there is God, and there is the gossip between them that the human ear eavesdrops upon; there is also the human, relations of body to body, and convolutions of heart to mind and mind to heart that understand love's reciprocity is a confounded, confounding form.

To do such work requires, as Guthrie knows, that one be at work also on oneself. This discovery can be harrowing, that even as "There I am—identifying," it is also true that "she found out she might be the inventor of herself." Such simultaneous concerns mark the deep ethical work this poet is invested in. To identify others—lover or God or shadow or sheet music or loneliness itself—one must also, and at the very same time, create the self capable of such work. The poem is the very place of such agonized efforts— not agony as in mere pain, but as in agon, that ground of pure struggle from which the gods themselves once emerged.

"To discern the soul," Guthrie writes, "there'd be a river in it." Note, reader, that even the soul, the portion of immortal being imagined so typically as one, unified, indivisible, is here a riven thing, something seeking a way to forge relation to itself so it might be connected to all that exists beyond, and what divides the self in two is a river: image of life's passing, river into which none can step twice.

To pay accurate attention is to find yourself broken in two, or more than two. It is to be shattered by the world you seek into a self comprised of many selves, a chorus, each with its own voice: gossip, other, priest, oracle, reader, and one unnamed because she has no name, I, by which I mean also anonymous. In these pages each speaks. Each listens. None is perfect; none is cast in a perfect light. Rather these dark, necessary lines lay tangent to each other, glance against one intensity only to err into different discovery, where the spiritual must grapple with the fact of the body, and where the body takes "the blame / for the deeds of the mind."

Guthrie writes a last line that doesn't illuminate all those that came before. Better, it holds within the various darknesses in which this book does its utmost work. "It was this kind of human," she says; and reader, I hear it thus: kind as type, and kind as adjective. This kind of human, this poet kind, gives us this kind book in which the difficulty we fear to admit that we are our own living example of will be tender to us even as we tend toward it, word by word, line by line, poem by poem, letting our vision adjust to the good dark.

Dan Beachy-Quick

unwitting

Let the will quietly and wisely understand that it is not by dint of labor on our part that we can converse to any good purpose with God, and that our own efforts are only great logs of wood laid on without discretion to quench this little spark . . .
—Saint Teresa of Avila

. . . the soul has no mouth . . .
—Saint Augustine

* weather'd

the world unwound, shut down

thunder, and a newly reckoned darkness

darkness makes the birds sound otherwise

the place inside, flushed out dark

wound up in sky crossed by lightning

holding the reigns of the visible

then visible: smells and calls

and other calls

shape gathering clouds

*

noise: even, every,
leaf, cloud, passing, reaches

even, under
darkness

silence can't be demonstrated
it has no edge

*

breaking what it needs,
digestion, the nourishment process

could be a good model

so on doors I pluck for sound, and out
of varying instruments

blender, mouth of bronze idol on mantle, mouth
color, interpret: vandalize:

*

vandal to rue

rues the day
rulers the dawn

maws dark tresses
the claws dark's ledges

*

and the others fussing bury the sound
they too are waiting

                c   a   w
                    c   a   w

the pitch a con

the con a cave
that begs an entrance

*

eyed-up surface — glimpses through black wrapping
a passing landscape — trees without heads — forest of stopped gestures

a passing head — tree without landscape — divested of posture
on the bank a beckoning — oily beak tied with ribbon —

one limb — a shovel — slinging sand in the direction of an eye —
from not being able to breathe to not being able to breathe

*

all birds are representative
and the scene impeccably lit

to hold the beak, stroke down,
the fabric

feel it up
feel it quit

*

what are you, crashed,
departed?

that stays around outside of heads
aloft, if not for chants

*

to discern the soul
there'd be a river in it

but by the bank, a shouter

shouting out sheet music
the chirp to wind

the shouter with mouth of blade
marking a target

*

dusk, grasses wind the hymn
silence is reverence

*

given everything
the give forms our lips

it's only the shape of zero

*

giving in
up, down

over over
what can hands bring in

what has no edge
it cannot visit

*

with vigil, I see outlines
are only choices made by eyes

like a river stepped in by mistake
I think to take you in

chorus

"God is near us, but we are far from Him, God is within, we are without, God is at home, we are in the far country."
—Meister Eckhart

*

dear missing,

a channel by land that gestures and juts, doesn't touch,

the water rushing shelters every sound I shout out into it,

the form of the shore is lost to the counting of sand,

the count is lost to the sound. If I could I'd

rearrange us! shove selves/shell letters/shelve us

(water, surfacing itself) inside ourselves

as "ever," as yours,

* the gossip

I don't always want what we have, she is saying.

Outside, dark clouds, fish hopping, tilling waves

back from shore. He is silent.

Sometimes more is happening, he says, finally.

The sun's coming up, she says. *Look how the light is kept.*

I'd like to keep it up, he says.

Don't make apart what is otherwise the same, he says.

She is silent, tilling shore back from shore.

Don't give darkness a face, he says, darkening.

* the others

I went to confession to sort out whom from whom.
The Priest as himself . . .
People in robes feel more walls,
so they probably know the openings.
Why don't you love him? he asked.
He's already kept, I said.
By whom? he asked.
Ideas, I said.
Mm. Maybe you can win him over.
There's too many of them, I said.
May you also be one in us, he said, reading from a text.

* the others

Let's take a walk at first light.

Light recollects tree
leaf into a spot.

There I am — identifying.

Are you afraid of you? I ask them. Because I am;
I always wish I would go, or someone would come.

Yes, we say. We are! Don't remind us.

* the priest

Imagine the Lord performs a test.
With one mirror, in an empty room: the entrance to his home.
And the call to his guests — *Come, I'm in the back,*
watching through a secret opening as they pass.

Imagine the whispers:
I don't care for submission. As much as coincidence.
And I'm not good at being very happy,
when not spoken to directly.

* the gossip

The tavern is damp, dark, filled with enough
to feel invisible. The Visible a violent character here.
She's tethered to a game. Man will play the ground.
What are you doing, protecting your rook? he'll say, taking the queen.
Trying to find a good place to hide, she'll say, letting him down.

* the reader

The spread reveals in threes —
Magician, Star and Liar.

Hands, light, and mouth
folded to contrive.

Smoke trying out the windowpane
lights rays trying in —

my hand is kept still
by my stance.

* the others

Outside, chirping because because because

ruling chance the conversation.

* the others

There is nothing to tell on the trees. Leaves leave bare air revealing.
A gossip is passing out functions by the river.
Others circle in raggedy reds and dirty yellows.
They too want to be told their role. *You two make orange*, the gossip sums.
She calls out my name as I hurry by, but I am devoted.
What do I give up, if I let the gossip in my house? I ask the oracle when I arrive.
One point-of-view may be avoided for many reasons, it says.
Give me two.
You want to hide or to tell more sides.
But of course, there are many characters!
Don't make your words a ribcage.

* the oracle

What can I make of Autumn?   *A given situation*
What is melancholy? *A formidable opponent, dressed sweetly*
What is nature? *A pocket*
sealed and torn Why
am I secret?*humble*
*are those made alone*What/
is modesty? *failure*
as landing, What is truth? *the truth*
we first forget
What should I do?
carry a breeze, or a cloud

* the gossip

She dreamed she was swimming out to sea,
curtain of black water, glistening,
forearms of waves heaving her further out —
let's go back in! she'd called, scared,
waved to shelve her self in:
Just remember to feed the family!
Life is putting on shows!
I have to pull on the curtains.

* the others

Sometimes it admits you its existence
shows the pose of curve it backs
sometimes noses a surface, quiet
enough, not to interfere

* the others

Late, empty for the rains

dark clouds and thundering,

seemingly little time.

What am I not seeing?

Shouting into the storm,

the empty places the disparate —

* the gossip

In alongside intuition a certain new loneliness creeps.

When she found out she might be the inventor of herself.

The light the word her eyes spill.

* the others

I wanted to know someone else who was a blur. All that came forth was a tear
in the fabric. To know my predicament —
do you have as much a sense of your face?

* the oracle

sometimes shadows become articulate

eyes that have the world

looking, a splinter
broken off inside

("my sight")

* the gossip

When she was a girl she was an inventor.
Lies would fly out her mouth, bright world, bright wings.
At first the children would flock to her like a colorful mother.
But then the room took on the other hue,
and feeling the feel of too-heavy wings, the too-heavy bird
fluttered and tottered and fell.

*the others

here, deepening its shadow: your feeling of awe

* the gossip

made up everything —
the stars the trees,
her own self

body

"So we must begin very near to go far. The near is where we are."
—J. Krishnamurti

*

behind the pupil

a floret of lines
burst toward release —

a question is raised

the body gives
its cross-hatched replies?

*

not knowing I came to find things colorful and kind
I in lawful cinders find, unkindred

one flower on the sill, wilting
just when the next is opening. naturally

fall to ash, the expectations, when

———

———

what wish & will will open the same time?
I ask the glass with a kind of dare —

the difference between fantasy and prayer
is innocence

*

what *ever* in the bloom?
what *never,* on what dream's shelf
is ever wilting?
on top the night's helm
my howling, starless
stark *ahems,* the tyrant *ahas* —
unmoored from port of stem,
thinkers keep their words

*

scarce is wonder
is wonder

the light in mind, a bloom,
deliberation? falls into

to unsheath leaf from vein
the question —

I see by the leaves what to do —
is raised?

*

what abyss this skinny body

from wonder springs

collecting selves in laws

(thought skipping rocks)

mind the road

that rounds the banks

keeps out pebblers . . .

*

to interrupt my reading again
I peel the pages off the covers to bath.

steam persuading, phrases frame
me. neck and knees — typefaced,

the arm reads
don't move yourself

the arm reads: *what keeps us apart*

the current pushes there
and back, there and back

a body in the bath

I don't move myself
I don't convince myself

*

put too many coins in gd
it doesn't play, and

then, if, still, or even
unplucked from the hook, and hung by

get me down, I'm upside down
trying the will,

riding it:

bones tell too much of life
to skin

*

behind all faces all bone
I saw in one moment an eye open

enough to soften the gaze,

in there should dare
weigh nothing

✳

walking days under ribcage
of oaks by the river

sometimes it oakens: you are in the body
of oak bones, other times whitens

in grimace, retrieves a perceiving,
or it could be a body it might be your body

in that case how silly all this time

*

dot to dot
to constellation, gown

trace its traces off again
finger the folds, star-lint

how the spaces they
flame up; lightspliced —

the robes fall; dark,

epilogue

"You are listening to Akasa . . . the dark which has no end"
—C. J. Koch, as quoted by Clark Coolidge

*

Belief in nothing collecting —
the lateness of hours,

sun in sea setting
light as face. Reflecting,

finding a sameness in things

the body took the blame
for the deeds of the mind

It was this kind of human

Acknowledgments

Thank you :

Tommaso Cioni, my heart, root and bone; Claudia Rankine, bone of the page;
Kim Young, the light inside. Thank you to generous readers, teachers, and friends:
Dan Beachy-Quick, Samantha Hunt, Brian Blanchfield, Eleanor Wilner, Ellen
Bryant Voigt, Alexandra Ashton. And thank you to Nancy, Charlie, Camron, and
Savannah, who *play the ground*, and to Olmo, who turned on the light of the earth.
Un ringraziamento particolare a Caterina Contin, Serena Ze Neri e Jacopo Parti.
Deepest gratitude and admiration for Jim Schley, Jeffrey Levine, Marie Gauthier,
and everyone at Tupelo Press.

Thank you also to the following journals for previously publishing poems or ver-
sions of poems from this book:

Cutbank: "the gossip" and "the oracle"

Drunken Boat: "and the others fussing, burying the sound," "behind all
faces all bone," "belief in nothing collecting," "put too many coins in gd," and
"what abyss our skinny body"

EOAGH: A Journal of the Arts: "If I speak," "what are you, thing," and
"what never in the bloom"

Fairy Tale Review: "made up everything," "nothing to tell," "not knowing,"
"of the oracle," "the tavern is damp," and "when she was a girl"

Omnidawn Omniverse: "dear missing," "the gossip," and "the reader"

Tarpaulin Sky: "weather'd"

Other books from Tupelo Press

See our complete list at www.tupelopress.org